Essential Tremor

01 02 03 04 05 25 24 23 22 21

Caitlin Press Inc.
8100 Alderwood Road,
Halfmoon Bay, BC V0N 1Y1
www.caitlin-press.com

Text and cover design by Vici Johnstone
Edited by David O'Meara
Printed in Canada

Caitlin Press Inc. acknowledges financial support from the Government of Canada and the Canada Council for the Arts, and the Province of British Columbia through the British Columbia Arts Council and the Book Publisher's Tax Credit.
Library and Archives Canada Cataloguing in Publication

Essential tremor : poems / by Barbara Nickel.
Nickel, Barbara, author.

Canadiana 20210095547 | ISBN 9781773860602 (softcover)
LCC PS8577.I3 E87 2021 | DDC C811/.54—dc23

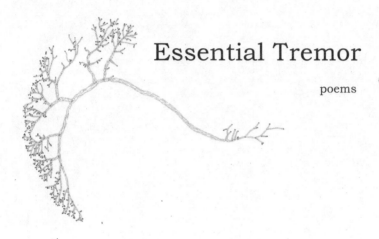

Essential Tremor

poems

Barbara Nickel

Caitlin Press 2021

For Bevan

It was not important that they survive.
What mattered was that they should bear
Some lineament or character,

Some affluence, if only half-perceived,
In the poverty of their words,
Of the planet of which they were part.

—Wallace Stevens, "The Planet on the Table"

Contents

Saskatoon to Coaldale, July, Highway   9
Angel Glacier, Mount Edith Cavell   10
Passport   11
Cyclist Killed in Collision on Highway 22   12
For Tim on His Fiftieth   14
Essential Tremor   15
Onychomycosis   16
Nickel Mines   17
Essential Tremor   18
Saskatoon to Edmonton, December, Train   19

Body in a Mirror   21

Corona   29

Anchoress (1)   43
Ear   44
Tongue   45
Uterus   46
Anchoress (2)   47
Hair   48
Spine   49
Anchoress (3)   50
Eyes   51
Hands   52

His something   55
Kitchen Maid with the supper at Emmaus   56
Nitinaht Lake   57
Postcard from Bonaire   59
Seven Last Words, Op. 51   60
Beethoven's Ninth (Finale)   67
From Beethoven's Autopsy   68
The Milk River   69
Bulbs   70
Hospital Room   71
Handsel   72
Five Years   73

Notes   75
Acknowledgements   78
About the Author   80

SASKATOON TO COALDALE, JULY, HIGHWAY

Not Winnifred the town we couldn't see.
The fox we weren't sure was a fox but might
have been if not a mutt. Not the way we—
the air-conditioning—not a fight
but cordially, frequently turning on and off.
Each farm lay more abandoned than the next
but curiously well-tended; neat but left.
There was a house we didn't pass that's fixed
itself nevertheless as seen by one looking
back—seen-through, its thin frame all pane-
less windows so it's that day—sun blinking,
light cloud and blue we're accustomed to, fine,
alone, impossibly far the porous house
as we drove on, impervious.

ANGEL GLACIER, MOUNT EDITH CAVELL

Your hanging
body
is not you
all
but spilled
ages ago from the hidden bowl
above when marmots hid in these caves
and do still.

But we can pretend
you've descended
to us on purpose,
that the turquoise
lake at your toe, my boy
denying his fear
of your calving's thunder
always will be,
pretend that you won't
in his lifetime
(almost sure)
shrink,
misshapen,
disappear.

July 2011

Passport

A sign in the corridor will lead
you to his room. It also leads
him to his room. (He's added
his mid-initial—P—with pen.
It irks him when the P is left behind.)

It's moving day, from Pineview Manor to
the west. Clear out the rancid butter, roll
the chesterfield away. (The west is where
you don't need furniture.) Where to, this cedar
chest? (It's guarding annals of a church

no longer there, baptisms kept in fine
Germanic script.) Where to, the family files,
the genealogies, this thin book?
(Next to his chest in Zanzibar, Calcutta,
Liechtenstein, Bombay, it opens

to a decade's travel. Linger—the streets
flutter with colour, flags hung for the great
festival, that ornate wooden door, bells
tolling in the dusk letting out
like a hem as a child hightails it across

the square; these pages lined with exits,
entries.) Bring it with the diapers and the clock
to admit its bearer (P intact) past
the tick-tock runway, docks, all moorings
recognizable or not, on the way to lost.

Cyclist Killed in Collision on Highway 22

Upon arrival, RCMP located a... cyclist deceased.

1. After a week, some of us wander the ditch grass just past Sunset Boulevard below the bent guardrail and incessant traffic.

2. After a time, disperse into a sad scavenger hunt.

3. Seat post, no seat.

4. Bottom bracket, clipless pedals connected to crank arms, chain rings askew.

5. One downtube made of carbon fibre so unexpectedly light. Hole where it had joined.

6. Thin, black smear on the tarmac before he flew. A few pace the grass for about 100 metres to where the pieces landed. He flew planes, too, knew their insides, took his daughters for rides.

7. In flight, his glove must have detached itself. Extra large for his helicopter-mending hands often bruised, callused, cut.

8. Crown, partial forks, brake.

9. These jagged craters cut from his white and red water bottle.

10. Earlier, the googled photo: line of larch above police cars and ambulance in the late afternoon. Although he didn't know it was his last view as he approached the downhill, did he gasp at the lit hills and yellow grass?

11. His cycling glasses, plastic, right lens with right arm still attached.

12. Rear derailleur.

13. Just the visor from his helmet.

14. Not one to gasp. He'd appreciate. Then thoughts of gears, a book, his next trip, where? But he'd have looked well at what we didn't see, now see, will see.

15. Ripped bits and pieces of carbon fibre torn as if a pocket's well-worn flannel.

16. Knowing the state of the driver, we calculate the SUV's approximate speed based on the distance covered by these parts.

17. Wells in us, welling.

18. What to do with these things.

19. Unharmed by a week of weather, not yet taken by the wind—condolence note with felt tip drawing—"…us kids should not witness nor should…" —signed anonymous.

October 2020

For Tim on His Fiftieth

Remember that July we spent alone
with Mom and Dad up at the lake? A month.
I didn't want to go. Fourteen. A loon
sounded my moods—impossible. Your tenth
birthday and you—content to fish and make
and look and chop and be—a distant species.
When I caved is hard to say but then the lake
and rock where I'd sulked became a piece
with us torquing through forest to the point
with string and Ritz and everything we needed
for our lean-to, not a house where at a point
in middle age we're looking back; but needle-
covered paths in the clearing
only here, ours in one particular summer.

Essential Tremor

Her shaking hands; he cuts her meat,
lifts and stows the tumblers (lipstick-stained,
dishwasher warm) and pulls the needle out
and pushes in the morphine for her migraines.
Essential is the car and God, the egg
farm's daily stench sent by the daily weather,
Trimipramine, Tim Hortons, there's a leg
of highway just a cinch, an easy half hour.
There's a drawer full of Hallmark cards,
each other's fondest wishes; the top one fresh
with embossed lilies from the anniversary
(their 51st) when, under her spoon collection,
he addressed himself, *Dear Dave, dear husband,*
signed *love* and her name in his steady hand.

Onychomycosis

Under the toenail, I see lights. Be gone
fungal mess; the bed has grown
its gloom over the months. I'll prescribe
the usual; pills, painless. Just scribble
it all back to piglet pink—yet—
the lights haunt. Pulse in the night
sky outside Edmonton when I stopped
the car. Got out numb—non-stop
from the coast. In hours it would be dawn.
Aurora shivered ghostspeak down,
waves, pale green parted, delivered
what—a cave, a heart? Something to live
by. And I thought (sagely, the ditch, firs,
highway, all that dark place concurred)
to drive on. Hello, industrial park, fire
of morning, tired diners, Canadian Tires,
flax, flax, flax, flax, flax,
hubs tacked on fences, ruined shacks, flocks
of reeling crows, prairie's fibre, root
and swing, slack of evening, backroad routes
and ruts not taken.
                    Hello, love. Her door
was open. Loaves of bread, still warm. I dared
to take her in my arms and not let go.
All night we rolled, twisted, writhed, glowed...
until morning; I was a body on a bed
knowing it would end.

Nickel Mines

Nickel Mines, Pennsylvania, October 2, 2006

You can't see
the small bones
of the five girls
who stopped
growing that day,
nor the worms
of their decay,
nor their mothers'
arms warm
around their killer's

beloved.
The eldest said
shoot me first,
stood in harm's
way unafraid of death
wearing
an apron, like
her mother,
baking bread
for the one
with the
handgun,
shotgun
and rifle.

Essential Tremor

If only it were that: a little
trembling in the hand. If we could tell
your leg be still and still it would. Be it-
self before we heard the news, reeling,
before the shift and the settle into our restless
bed, the shudder as you roll—
here and gone and here momentous
as aurora and nothing I can hold.
Ends always with me spoon-feeding
and push-chairing, the secret life
of drool which maybe isn't half so bad as it looms;
in our room would gather the minuscule
beauties, for instance wind flickering the aspen,
every quaver I'm given from your hand.

Saskatoon to Edmonton, December, Train

The town we used to visit is almost buried
in the dark. Pick out the rink and boarded
station, exhaust haloing an idling car.
Pick out the train's bell flattening the more
we move away—now we're the scene we saw
last winter from the road although
a year ahead and how far west who knows.
Midnight in the dome car: time enough
it seems, until the morning we arrive
then barely stop until another year
has passed. November is a train of cars
down the road spewing gravel and clearing
for once that night, town, its frosty ghosts; the one
we used to visit there is gone.

BODY IN A MIRROR

From notes by Leonardo da Vinci accompanying his musculo-skeletal drawings in his "Anatomical Manuscript A." These were written from right to left, as in a mirror.

I have looked

from
outside from inside

~~from~~
~~outside~~ from
behind

~~from outside~~
from outside

from
inside.

1. The Muscles of the Upper Spine

Begin with a perfect
man, then draw him
less, stripping
him in stages
down
to the bone
and this will be
a most beautiful
diagram.

2. The Bones, Muscles and Tendons of the Hand

Which is the cause
of the tightening
which is strongest
and thickest
what is it that bends
the bone
that bends
the finger
how the nerves
penetrate I am
constrained
I say the thing will give
pain.

3. The Muscles of the Face and the Arm, and the Nerves and Veins of the Hand

Have you seen here
the diligence of
nature,
muscle of anger,
muscle bigger
because it has to
endure,
muscle of sorrow,
muscle for biting,
muscle of anger.

4. The Muscles and Tendons of the Lower Leg and Foot

The foot in all its beauty,
bones sawn through,
transparent,

seen.

5. The Bones of the Hand

The hand held
as a clenched fist.

Hand that shows
the inner side.

6. The Muscles of the Leg

Lean
and thin
muscles.

Space
arises
between
one
and
the other makes

a
window.

7. The Muscles of the Shoulder and Arm

The furthest
movements of the
edges:

the uvula,
the tongue,

the last molars.

Each one on its own
naked on the bone,
seeing its
beginning
and end
with lines
alone.

8. The Vertebral Column

Immense.　　Immense.

Corona

1 (And so)

And so begins its reign (google to see its crown
under a microscope). Infected prince.
Infected star. And so begins your cancelled
life (infected wife). And over there half-mast is flown
(they load the coffins into trucks). And so
begins shopping with gloves (your mother over
there and when you'll get to her is never
maybe); talking through screens, and so and so—

And I lie awake with itchy hands.
And tenderize the meat with hammered blows.
And when we'll meet and touch nobody knows.
And so we live by stats and rules and ands.

That rooster down the tracks
pecking, oblivious.

March 30, 2020

2 (Safeway)

Pecking, oblivious,
the Safeway crows construct in blooming trees
what's theirs. What's ours? Try not to seize
the toilet paper please. One each. Whereas
this homeless guy and the queen (immaculate
in green) get less and more and more and less.
But take a look at Boris, the virus
doesn't discriminate (it does).

And how much Easter chocolate should I get?
And should I fill my cart until it's filled?
Southeast of here a potter's field is filled
and let me out of here, I want to get
into my car, in safety watch this blessed
family working, twining twigs into a nest.

April 11, 2020

3 (Spring)

Family working, twining twigs into a nest;
cherry, trillium, corona bloom
while that buffoon condemns the WHO; on Zoom,
inside, outside, in danger zones, the rest
battle the king of everywhere
who won't allow a service for the dead
and sneaks noiseless into the lungs, is dread
on surfaces but strangely isn't tearing

us apart; we will receive their surplus
masks, we are arriving at the ends
of paragraphs and meals; that wending
of the river the evening he surprised us—
dark swath, a log until it gleamed—
a beaver dived into the running stream.

April 18, 2020

4 (News)

A beaver dived into the running stream
that became river, estuary, strait, a sea
that made a fog that hid a strain that came to be
the news—old news. It replicates, like rhyme,
with slight changes: a home is hit, old people
die. Then him. Almost a century,
from Hamilton by way of Sicily
and then it's him. A nurse's phone took people

to his side. FaceTime: maybe my uncle
heard my violin. Alone he was
and wasn't. It was him. Amid the chaos
of the news I heard the news he
died. Turned on the news. Care home, virus.
That body on the gurney could be his.

April 25, 2020

5 (Until)

That body on the gurney could be his,
his body's journey to an urn the sun
will warm until—until. Not soon
the service. Gather not, until. Selfish,
you wish a crowded ship, haircuts, a trip
across the border or those boring golden days
you'd have people over. This is a phase
you tell yourself, beating the overripe
bananas into bread, shaping a poem
into the closet where you write, the lines
contained by laundry, a slight desk, aligned
by rules of close and far; windowless home,
we collide, overlap. Where is the unveil,
a way we can be us again until—

May 2, 2020

6 (Doctor)

A way we can be us again until
we can be us again depends on a curve
she worried early into flattening (her
pause; the track on her cheek for the frail,
the numbers weighing, unsleeping her,
delivered without fail, in measured tones
what can't be measured; for even one
how evenly she suffers).

Sales suffering too. I watch the antics
of a southern foil (unlikely foil
but even so) and, equally, the circles
under her eyes, wonder if as a girl she ever picked
a dandelion globe and almost blew it to the wind—
stopped herself, sheltered with her hand.

May 11, 2020

7 (Lack)

Stopped herself. Sheltered with her hand.
I mean from crying out. I mean she hid
her finger black from work. I made
that up with facts from the report but our ground
beef she picked for bones is true. And that she died
from you know what a day after officials said
that place was safe. Condolences not said
until the news revealed the lack and the lie.

The sky above the Taj Mahal is blue.
The Louvre emptier for all the life it's held.
Great halls are vast with music never heard.
And vast the time I haven't spent with you.

Her husband works there too, when asked
said he felt numb (translated, speaking through a mask).

May 17, 2020

8 (Cover)

Said he felt numb. Translated, speaking through a mask,
her husband said he'd caught it too, and, speaking
through a mask, my husband in the parking lot pokes
a swab into a patient's nose, and, fumbling with his mask,
his father plants the beans,
his hair white with silver, mask handsewn, yellow chicks and pale
green fish, he stoops to sow the kale,
adjusts his mask, kneeling, leaning.

Kids on bikes but mostly quiet on our street.
Our grass, our hair is clipped, the rose climbs
almost in ordinary time,
it pricks my thumb for blooms, it's sweet

before: ho-hum, we're getting on a plane,
on our way to... (nothing will be the same).

May 26, 2020

9 (Ghost)

On our way to nothing will be the same:
Detroit, July of '67, on the list
of the deceased, the four-year-old hit
by the National Guard after a sniper in her home.
The same as this, we watched a city burn.
She'd be about my age. We're on a plane
(with masks, two seats between) above the same
tumult: *It was my life. You didn't learn.*

On our way to nothing will be the same
is the procession of the dead. In motels, on the gallows,
at intersections they come and go, vow
they're dead and can't breathe; let nothing be the same.

The airport quiet as a crypt.
She walks ahead. We don't touch yet.

June 15, 2020

10 (Essential)

She walks ahead. We don't touch yet
except this place within—my phone, her scroll
and fingerboard not skin but living, set
under her chin for life. She plays although
her audience has scattered into screens.
She plays alone. It's night. She offers
us her home—the fire escape a ladder leans
against in chips of light, herself
at work beside the bed. I said she walks,
walks in music, climbs each step practised
since she was three, here's breath, talk,
meal, the wine, the world, the window, listen
to each solitary rafter lift. Outside: off-kilter
boards on a frame, a hose and pail in shadow.

June 27, 2020

11 (Travel)

Boards on a frame, a hose and pail in shadow,
summer day like all the others, hot
without a cloud. For a picnic why not
pretend on Zoom. Each day the dew,
weeding, watering. A barbecue.
No one comes inside. The dill
looks fried. Rotting prawns, the maggots killed,
practise your instrument for what. Blue
day after day after the panic. Still
numbers. Our dying
fridge. TikTok. Netflix. The news is trying
to be new and the marigold, ruffled
sentry, kneel for its spice
to let you find another place and shadow.

August 8, 2020

12 (Door)

To let you find another place and shadow,
hollow in my old backyard, before
the summer's gone, let's set out before dawn
to get the sun and mist past Hope. I know
the route. You whistle, off and on. Hours
allow us the braided streams and blackbird, ditch garbage, wet faces
of rock, paintbrush, wild vetch and, after a day, a glacial
snout too far away, discharging milky water. *Rock flour*
I say as if I still know more than you.
Doritos on the floor. Even at night the wheat
stays waiting near where your grandpa hated
picking rocks from the soil and now he's moving
toward the door to us—
I wish. We can't. Too dangerous.

September 10, 2020

13 (Smoke)

It was evening all afternoon.
—Wallace Stevens

I wish. We can't. Too dangerous
to go out there. Hardly war yet
we're wary, weary: beware creosote,
crowds, particles, something monstrous
in a bar, lung. Is this spread from far for real,
the sun a slip of manna, orange-tinged,
that ridge of trees as if in snow? If a hinge
could creak us back—but no. Real

snow once stung my wrists under wet wool
mitts. In this mist (it isn't mist) beginnings end where ends
begin so when (despite warnings) you run the river loop, minding
the obstacles, roots, you almost miss the owl

from the cottonwood, soft call, seer of what it doesn't own.
And so begins its reign (google to see its crown).

September 25, 2020

ANCHORESS (1)

You ask me what I've given up: outside.
Need I elaborate? Foxgloves for one,
the way I'd let my finger slide
into its freckled mitt, the honey
there. Wherever rain reaches—listening
to it against the pane or witnessing a squall
isn't the same as drizzle loose
on my skin, autumn, its elegant fall
into the dark. Here I live divided
into prayers. Matins and sext. Vespers.
Compline. Apple is sin, round and red
I've plucked and thrown away for Him who whispers
to me on my bed. My love is *Christ...*
who was alive as is the tender eye.

EAR

Luke 22:50-51

Consider the ear
in the olive grove,
speed of the sword

whirring
                        fear,
olive leaves,
bleeding sound.

Sever hammer.
Sever love—

When sound has fled
(blather uttered
in the olive grove,
                        —how bad?
what said?)

But the
          inner chambers
                        (at a party, in the bright piazza)
will receive the waves
                                    travelling
all presumed dead

          dizzying, lovely (servant's
servant

          silent).

Tongue

John 8:3-6

Tongue-No-Tongue

> (*What tongue can frame… ?*)

what bride-no-bride
>>> no bridle?

You sit
and write.

What word?

Word, what
bid them bite
their tongues?   —*Tongues*

in tongs! (Shame on—) Flames
to words
and pride
and idle
sitting, whittling.

>>> —*A little bird told me.*
>>>> —*What?*
>>> —*Burned them, then*

quiet.

(*No tongue, no*
tongue, no…)

Tongue—

> (*The Word became…*)

become…

UTERUS

Luke 1:39-41

Feels like crap,

         craves apples

Twinkies, is ever

            peeing

                ever

                    fat.

        —You'll never
        recover.

Kneeling,
throwing up...

(*...found favour...*)   *—What crap!*

(*...in a twinkling...*)   *—You believe*
that? Get rid
of it
slut.

Where fools rove (kneeling to stand up)

on the brink
         —Save her!
she greets—

(where hills are level and a
cover reveals rivers
of sap from hapless
inkless Never)

           ever fruit
(*...from the root...*)

My love,
    alive—

ANCHORESS (2)

Our Rule instructs: *In bed, do not do or think*
of anything but sleep. But sleep eludes.
My crucifix at night becomes anything—
a kind of crossroads where guests including
Our Lady pass. She has small breasts, her thighs
are thin like mine but inside us is the vastest
stretch of anything I can't describe—
to call it sweet robs it of pain. Is Christ
in it, I've asked, and think perhaps, where shallow's
deep; our navel crowns His dome; a kiss
sets off an earthquake in the smallest hall
and in is out, in prison is release.
The rooster crows. Get dressed.
Kneel for lauds. Confess.

Hair

Luke 7:36-38

i.

Plucks a
chicken   lily
one grey hair
                fear from the gut
of her guitar

Chucks
            merkin silks
her junk her wares
now bonfire
now bare

Down the sidewalk
shaking
                —Tail!
with her jar
with her hair
with her
                —Such a career!

ii.

Tears drench a toe
                —Follow the trail
the rarest overflow
                        falls
through the air

                (*... And lo...*)
—A veil

all she can bare

—Show me
                                Halley's tail
                        here
            the star
                    pouring
        her

SPINE

Luke 13:10-16

i.

Dog Rose
of the Twisted-Spine.

How came she in

       Here?

Up yours
up the sacral
up
Halo Row
she goes

dangerous to the Crest,

the Promontory
                coming
into our in, in

       Here.

ii.

A whipping is yours.

(*Up*—)

             A whipping, a thistle
crown   (*Crawl*
            up—)

and smell of wild dog

Wild Briar Rose

rising—

Anchoress (3)

Our Rule instructs: *Therefore, dear sisters, love*
your windows as little as you possibly can.
I've tried to hate the holes through which travel
my soup, the blessed chamber pot, canticles
and psalms, smells from visitors—some yarrow-
laden bank, a herd of hogs. Inward
I go, searching for Christ. He isn't there.
The room is empty except for me, awkward,
unlovely in my limbs, trying to pray.
The curtain flutters my uncertainty.
I pull it back, like opening an eye—
one dingy courtyard, rag of sky but seeing
magnifies my cell into the world
for which I magnify the Lord.

EYES

John 9:6-11

Gutter, rubble,
litter

        am I...

        —Not fit.

—So be it!

        —What's what

inscribed,
taught

                        see-sees
                        what's right.

        (Shit and dirt, godspit, gobs
        of it on
                Old-Eyes
        in the twilight...)

What
lifting, lit?

What—

        —Slob!

infinite I-

        —Out!

ris-
es...

HANDS

John 20:24-25

Mister Conjuror, render
your hands.
                  Not remembering
but bones, tendons
                      in spring—

                                        Lost

Master…

Worst-Fear Vendor
                  rending the curtain
                  (*gone*
is
bearing),

you must
(*no metaphors*)
deliver

hands
            tending
bending

open
         palms
                bursting
                (*burrs, sting*)
spring—

His something

spilled—seed,
stones, lake
of foam, wind,
beast, lupine field
and it was good,
a secret
feast, a slaking
no one
saw.

A committee
called it sin, after
which pleasure
was confined to
under
things—a fold
of skin could never
hills, a skin of snow
was slime.

I say all this
because I saw
you at fourteen
slipping your things
into the wash
and heard you ask
"And did our Saviour
ever that when
loneliness?"

Kitchen Maid with the supper at Emmaus

Diego Velázquez, c. 1618. Oil on canvas.

She scrubs. Listens.
Clutches the ear
of the jug. The garlic
had been hard to peel.

Oh well for ages since,
Christ in the dim
next room murmuring
to men. One owner

has him painted over
but underneath he breaks
the bread she's punched
down warm and risen

by the pot always
about to fall, bowls
upside-down because
she's placed them ump-

teen times that way,
each dish empty
except the jug she may
have filled and may bring

in, pouring, know
him as her own
a moment before
he's air.

NITINAHT LAKE

with gratitude to the Ditidaht First Nation Community

Our first son
before he could speak
watched the water as from nothing
whitecaps appeared
and lifted your sail
to thirty knots.

We'd seek
the Northern Cross
within the wings
and breast of Cygnus
the Swan, six stars
inside a myth eclipsed
by spit-up and teething.
Later connect the dots

to conjure a swan's nervous
system, nails on the cross,
twinkling eyes, etc.
A diagram. A power *out there*,
I will lift up mine eyes, etc.

The fire's
snuffed into the pebbled
beach. Your nervous
system begins
to fail. Or a grimmer
blow—a friend
who stargazed, ate chips
in the next lawn chair, to suffer
a violence
we can't know—
from whence
cometh my help?

Sometimes in the tent
is all. Unzip
my jeans, we make
a little cross
of two, wind
and woodsmoke, the baby
near, unlocking
milk and care.

Postcard from Bonaire

Here lies a coast
with postcard slaves
harvesting postcard
salt in wheelbarrows,
piles of it like mashed
potatoes, please
pass the salt.

Rows of slave huts
painted orange to match
the obelisk that
told merchant
ships far off what grade
of salt was here.
You rare and precious

salary,
you centrepiece
unseen in the broth
in the body, the paths
to you
in the forest
where the deer come

to lick. Here
are afternoons
too hot for anything
but on my knees
inside a hut so small and plain
it could be for a dog;
here lies a coast of tears.

Seven Last Words, Op. 51

for Ian Hampton

Sonata I in B-flat major

His body is a tapestry of scars.
Beaten with green bamboo. Hung by his thumbs.
Knuckles burned with cigarettes. The rack.
That winter night near Naumberg when a human
isn't but an it turned into ice
by the boys, whose fingertips we kissed when they
were babies, little dears, before they touched
a trigger. Playing a cello string saying
forgive. Oh no, not that, we can't,
so in ancient manuscripts his bloody words
from Luke were just left out. *No sir we ain't*
in heaven yet the hanging man's a coward.
So backwards forwards inside out his gorgeous
resonance—resistance—is ignored.

Sonata II in C minor (ending in C major)

Witch Hazel

It makes no sense. A host of hairy blooms
in January of all things. Twinges
of scent where empty air should be. Limbs
laden with light when ours and hers are dirge.
She died last night. Stop plucking. Keep C minor
to the end, then end. Impossible
this colour in the cold and criminals
in paradise, whisper from the rabble,
almost dead, of going on. It makes
no sense but there it is under your ear
each spring, the whirring habitat from bleak
nothing and in the final bars
a small bird against all odds finds nectar
at our tree, communion here.

Sonata III in E major

To My Son

Tone inside tone. We were that close, we rose
as one. I felt you pushing off to swim, a quaver
in our cave. Sometimes I'd miss
your heart, ahead by half a beat—you'd leave,
I knew. The playground noise. You were there.
I was here. It got worse; you'd shut
me out. I drove to work, didn't hear
from you it seemed for years. Forgive the hurt
you bear and bore, each all of that resolves
into a fresh dissonance, resolve
into a word, a room where we can live
again. Not marble, you on my lap, that love,
but this: kingdom of listening, ear
asks from within, what sorrow.

Sonata IV in F minor

This music keeps dissolving into air
the way a friend was here and then was not.
These bars of rest—not absence but a rare
attention given to the elfin notes
descending from a violin of ancient
wood; the listening of trees.

Where are you? Lost or dead or missing, bent
under a cruelty—

           ||: In Paris, rosin
taken from the cases of musicians
sent to camps was stored in cartons. :|| Rosin
taken from the stumps of pines. The sickly
powder of all suffering is you
incarnate on the horsehair in the whimper
of my *why* dissolving into air.

Sonata V in A major

So simple in A major: run the tap
until it's cool, then drink—it's mostly free—
then dump. Vinegar brought to the lips
on a stalk of hyssop is for the girl who flees,
on her eight-hour trek to the puddle, a man
who will rape her. *O Hart after the water
brookes and deepe to deepe the noyse.* We run
to raise money for her and satisfy
our thirst from plastic bottles, never free.
Above the plick, plick, a keening
over, over, then inside; the phrase
that didn't die with him who was caned,
the least of these, I thirst, *Ich durste,*
I thirst, *i'nae Temptognal,* I thirst...

Sonata VI in G minor (ending in G major)

Grinding of C at D flat—he chose to sail
back home to the ghastliness it had become.
He spoke when he should not. He chose to rail
against his country's rules; they hated him.
He suffered execution. We know all this,
what choices cost. But Haydn in the night
changing the key, sounding bliss after bliss,
marking the stillness of the dead with notes
gliding unseen, no scars in sight. The noose
is cleaned by a guard shaking his head. The dawn
is stuck with hundreds of barbed wire crosses
held in place by thick posts; another gone.
He said in prison there had been a thrush
loosing all it was into the hush.

Sonata VII in E-flat major (and Conclusion)

Haydn

Does a spirit depart muted, afraid, alone
like me, the boy whose linen voice had split
between two whole notes in the choir? I was thrown
out—no coins, three shirts, a threadbare coat.
Thinner yet the spirit runs—where?
Leaky garret without a stove. I lived
to play my worm-eaten spinet and married
music, envied no king. I believe
that every note has been preparing me
to write this last sonata for Our Lord's
last breath when the Holy veil—a mystery—
was torn away and how the music pours
like the rain that night when the cast-out boy
stepped so lightly into the street—terrible joy.

Beethoven's Ninth (Finale)

Withdrawing from view as sound withdrew,
he'd stick a pencil in his mouth to touch
the piano's soundboard and through
it meet vibrations on his tongue—note, clash, clutch
of cellos, rumble, a flute, brass, echoes
the faintest tiptoe away—his shrivelling
ears in the marsh, on the margins, the way he'd wreck
pianos, bashing keys to hear. Yet—*receive ... this kiss.*

Bliss this night; they're dancing in the streets.
A rupture, rapture, a melody of ballots
cast from silence, voices heard, those false tweets
can't change the change the people wrought.

Ode over, onstage, back turned, music, pulse;
the grateful crowd is mute to him, already somewhere else.

November 2020

From Beethoven's Autopsy

March 27, 1827

1. The external ear was large and irregularly formed, especially the concha was very spacious and half as large again as usual: the various angles and sinuosities were strongly marked.

2. The external auditory canal was covered with shining scales, the tympanum concealed by them.

3. The Os petrosum traversed by vessels of considerable size.

4. The auditory nerves, shriveled and destitute.

5. The convolutions of the brain were full of water, and remarkably white; they appeared very much deeper, wider, and more numerous than ordinary.

6. The liver appeared shrunk up to half its proper volume, of a leathery consistence and greenish-blue color, and was beset with knots, the size of a bean, on its tuberculated surface.

7. The Pancreas was equally hard and firm, its excretory duct being as wide as a goosequill.

8. Both Kidneys were invested by cellular membrane of an inch thick, and infiltrated with a brown turbid fluid; every one of their calices was occupied by a calcareous concretion of a wart-like shape and as large as a split pea. The body was much emaciated.

9. (Signed) Dr. Joseph Wagner
       Assistant in the Pathological Museum

The Milk River

isn't milk nor sweet
the Sweetgrass Hills.
The hoodoos don't

reply or call or what
you will when a friend
turns

off the highway
to suicide. They are not
answering why

or why.
But the cool
river oh

will taste you,
take you
who knows where
to ride.

BULBS

Dark day in the rain laid in:
scilla, tulipa,
himalaicus, narcissus...

Jessica—
    who brought you in?
—tulipa, scilla,
in dens the faceless

as earth, the year, closes in.
Spill of bonemeal,
            flow of pills—

                        Jesus
you're pale, who knows you're in?
Tamp down, lock up,
water, noiseless—

the bed is done and dark, go in.

Make tea, make beds,
soup, upstairs sleep

as layers

beneath
                        they're
there.

In spring they flare.

Hospital Room

after Margaret Avison's "New Year's Poem"

Chill and old. Rain thrashes the window,
almost seems to enter in. No nurses
come and Nicola is snoring, fallen
earphones leaking rock 'n' roll, faint glow

and purr, drip and beep of our machines
while the woman in the corner murmurs
in her sleep. Balloons the children gave
to Mrs. Wong bob and lean

over her retching; in procession her grave-
faced relatives left long ago. Except one,
perhaps her sister, who tucks, at the foot
of my bed, over my feet and in her grief,

by the stone ledge and the ill-fitted
panes letting in long trains
of dark space hastening
from out there—comfort,

a blanket, hard won here. And that almost
inaudible hum, breath under breath, lines ever-
looping in the dim light of what is and has been,
is yet to come—I believe
                that's Margaret

(she died last month), working on syntax.

Handsel

for Christopher Patton and Stephanie Bolster

A book
that fits in the palm
like a rhizome of ginger
or hops, mixing its vellum,
minutes, pixels, crumb
trail of laughter fed
from actual bread
kneaded before the war
when words were known
by heart and no one
knew the art
of plugging in.

Or a Negroni
by a woman
in a black dress whose
husband did her hair, stirred
in the clockless life
of ravens, a necessary
cache
reached ever more
infrequently
at best.

Nevertheless to be delivered
any year now as sand
and wrinkles meet
on the upper lip.

We pass it evenly from hand to hand.

FIVE YEARS

for Elise Partridge (1958-2015)

This grief, aging, hasn't grown old:
your open book still on my desk;
the servant mends, copies sold
while this grief ages, doesn't grow old
inside, a dwelling never filled,
the garden still, alone at dusk
with grief still green as old
as the stone in your book on my desk.

NOTES

"Cyclist Killed in Collision on Highway 22": The title and epigraph are from an article by the same title in *CochraneTODAY.ca* (October 1, 2020).

"Body in a Mirror": Da Vinci's original notes and their English translations are published with the drawings in Martin Clayton's and Ron Philo's *Leonardo da Vinci: The Mechanics of Man* (Los Angeles: Getty Publications, 2010).

"Corona 10 (Essential)": I owe a debt of gratitude to Chloe Kim's "Musical Offering" on the Early Music Vancouver website, which includes her performance of Nicola Matteis Jr.'s "Alia Fantasia," a photograph by Alec Jacobson, and Chloe's words about her situation.

"Corona 13 (Smoke)": The epigraph by Wallace Stevens is from "Thirteen Ways of Looking at a Blackbird." On September 24, 2020, *The New York Times* reported that in the 2020 wildfire season, over five million acres had been burned in California, Oregon and Washington. Millions on the coast spent weeks living under thick clouds of smoke and ash.

"Anchoress": All italicized words are quotations from *Ancrene Wisse*, also referred to as the "Anchoresses' Guide," written in Middle English sometime between 1225 and 1240, a book of religious instruction for three sisters of noble birth who had themselves sealed into cells for life as anchoresses somewhere between Worcester and Wales. The author is thought to have been a Dominican friar or Augustinian canon.

"Ear," "Tongue," "Uterus," "Hair," "Spine," "Eyes," "Hands": These poems comprise a biblical palimpsest and use a formal pattern—"sound scaffolding"— generated by consonance. Instead of forming stanzas by rhyme pattern, these poems move by a looser arrangement of repeated sound clusters based on the words' final consonants, as shown in the following example from "Ear":

Stanza 1

Consider (**r**) the ear (**r**)
in the olive (**v**) grove (**v**),
speed (**d**) of the sword (**d**)

Stanza 2

whirring (**r**)

        fear (**r**), etc.

"Tongue": "What tongue can frame" is a phrase from a hymn text by Isaac Watts. The phrase "Burned them, then/quiet" refers to Hopkins abandoning poetry and burning his early verse when he entered the Jesuit Order in 1868. "The Word became..." refers to John 1:14: "And the Word was made flesh, and dwelt among us..." (King James Version).

"Eyes": The term "Old-Eyes" is from Margaret Avison's "Early Easter Sunday Morning Radio."

"Nitinaht Lake": The italicized lines are from Psalm 121 (King James Version).

"Seven Last Words, Op. 51": Seven phrases attributed to Jesus during his crucifixion, used often in Good Friday Services since the sixteenth century. Joseph Haydn's *Seven Last Words, Op. 51*—a string quartet work with a movement composed for each phrase—was published in 1787. The phrases are from the following references—Sonata I, Luke 23:34; Sonata II, Luke 23:43; Sonata III, John 19:26-27; Sonata IV, Matthew 27:46; Sonata V, John 19:28; Sonata VI, John 19:30; Sonata VII, Luke 23:46.

"Sonata I in B-flat major": "His body is a tapestry of scars," Nancy Macdonald, "His Brother's Keeper," *Maclean's* (24 April 2015). The phrase "...when a human/isn't but an it, an ice to teach/the boys..." is after a scene from Anthony Doerr's *All the Light We Cannot See*.

"Sonata IV in F minor": ||: :|| Musical notation meaning to repeat the phrase within. "In Paris..." is after a detail from W.G. Sebald's *Austerlitz*.

"Sonata V in A major": "O Hart..." is after Psalm 42 (King James Version, 1611). *Ich durste* and *i'nae Temptognal* translate as "I thirst" in German and Amharic respectively.

"Sonata VII in E-flat major (and Conclusion)": "I envied no king his lot" and "...my old, worm-eaten spinet," words of Haydn, noted by Georg August Griesinger, one of Haydn's first biographers.

"Beethoven's Ninth (Finale)": The words in italics are from Friedrich Schiller's "Ode to Joy," the choral text for the Finale of Beethoven's Symphony No. 9. "Receive this embrace, you millions! This kiss is for the whole world!" is an excerpt from a translation used in a performance by the Chicago Symphony Orchestra (May 7, 2015). At the premiere of the symphony on May 7, 1824, the audience applauded as onstage Beethoven, completely deaf, still conducted.

"From Beethoven's Autopsy": Found from Beethoven's autopsy in *Thayer's Life of Beethoven* by Alexander Wheelock Thayer, revised and edited by Elliot Forbes (Princeton: Princeton University Press, 1964).

"Handsel": The word "handsel" (noun and verb) was dropped from the second (latest) edition of the *Canadian Oxford Dictionary*.

Acknowledgements

I'm deeply grateful to Stephanie Bolster and Christopher Patton for a decade plus years of sustained dedication to these poems and the manuscript as a whole, which would not exist as it does without their care. I owe a huge debt of gratitude to David O'Meara, a superb and generous editor at just the right time. I'm grateful to the late Elise Partridge for invaluable critiques and support. Thanks to Vici Johnstone, Sarah Corsie, Monica Miller and others at Caitlin Press for all the commitment and dedication involved in turning my manuscript into a book. For generosity, insight, information and support, thanks also to Katia Grubisic, Ian Hampton, Mark Klassen, Maurice Mierau, Stephen Partridge and Robert Thiesen.

Much gratitude goes to Lois Klassen and the late Heinz Klassen for generously sharing a space where many of these poems were written, and to Heinz for his design of a new space. Thanks to all of my family and friends for patience, love and support.

Thanks to the editors of the following publications in which these poems appeared, sometimes in earlier versions:

Alhambra Poetry Calendar 2010: "Bulbs"

Arc Poetry Magazine: "Essential Tremor" (Her shaking...)

Center for Mennonite Writing Journal (*mennonitewriting.org*): "Nickel Mines," "Postcard from Bonaire"

The Cresset: "Postcard from Bonaire"

CV2: "Tongue," "Hair," "Glacier," "From Beethoven's Autopsy"

Event: "Ear," "Hands," "Spine," "Uterus"

The Fiddlehead: "The Milk River"

The Malahat Review: "Anchoress (1), (2), (3)," "Hospital Room," "Passport"

subTerrain: "Corona: 1(And so), 2 (Safeway), 3 (Spring), 4 (News), 5 (Until)"

The Walrus: "Essential Tremor" (If only...), "Onychomycosis," "Saskatoon to Coaldale, July, Highway"

Winnipeg Review (*winnipegreview.com*): "Eyes"

"Essential Tremor" (Her shaking...) and "Saskatoon to Coaldale, July, Highway" were published in *Naked in Academe: Celebrating 50 Years of Creative Writing at UBC*, ed. Rhea Tregebov (McClelland & Stewart, 2014).

About the Author

BEVAN VOTH PHOTO

Essential Tremor is Barbara Nickel's third collection of poetry. Her first collection, *The Gladys Elegies*, won the Pat Lowther Award and her second, *Domain*, was a *Quill & Quire* Best Book of the Year. Nickel's work has appeared in many magazines and anthologies including *The Walrus*, *Poetry Ireland Review*, *Arc Poetry Magazine*, and *The Malahat Review*. Nickel is also an author of books for young people, one of which won a BC Book Prize and was shortlisted for the Governor General's Award and the Canadian Library Association Book of the Year. Her other children's titles have been nominated for the Ruth and Sylvia Schwartz Children's Book Award, as well as several Young Readers' Choice awards. Barbara Nickel lives and writes in Yarrow, BC.